MORE LIGHTS ON YOGA

SRI AUROBINDO

More Lights on Yoga

SRI AUROBINDO ASHRAM
PONDICHERRY

First Edition 1948
Fourth Edition 1983
Fourth Impression 2001

ISBN 81-7058-277-6

© Sri Aurobindo Ashram Trust 1948, 1983
Published by Sri Aurobindo Ashram Publication Department
Printed at Sri Aurobindo Ashram Press, Pondicherry
PRINTED IN INDIA

These are mostly extracts from letters written by Sri Aurobindo to his disciples in answer to their queries. Wherever possible the letters have been reproduced at length or even in full, in order to preserve their charm and spontaneity. Written over a period of many years (mostly during the 1930s), they have been put together and arranged in sections in the manner of *Lights on Yoga* so as to be of help to aspirants for the understanding and practice of yoga.

CONTENTS

CONTENTS

GOAL AND AIM

The aim of the Yoga is to open the consciousness to the Divine and to live in the inner consciousness more and more while acting from it on the external life, to bring the inmost psychic into the front and by the power of the psychic to purify and change the being so that it may become ready for transformation and in union with the Divine Knowledge, Will and Love. Secondly, to develop the Yogic consciousness, i.e., to universalise the being in all the planes, become aware of the cosmic being and cosmic forces and be in union with the Divine on all the planes up to the Overmind. Thirdly, to come into contact with the transcendent Divine beyond the Overmind through the supramental consciousness, supramentalise the consciousness and the nature and make oneself an instrument for the realisation of the dynamic Divine Truth and its transforming descent into the earth-nature.

*

I do not know that there is anything like a Purushottama consciousness which the human being can attain or realise *for himself*; for, in the Gita, the Purushottama is the Supreme Lord, the Supreme Being who is beyond the Immutable and the Mutable and contains both the One and the Many. Man, says the Gita, can attain the Brahmic consciousness, realise himself as an eternal portion of the Purushottama and live in the Purushottama. The Purushottama consciousness is the consciousness of the Supreme Being and man by loss of ego and realisation of his true essence can *live in* it.

*

1. Loss of egoism – including all ambition (even "spiritual" ambition), pride, desire, self-centred life, mind, will.
2. Universalisation of the consciousness.
3. Absolute surrender to the transcendental Divine.

*

There can be no mental rule or definition. One has first to live in the Divine and attain to the Truth – the will and awareness of the Truth will organise the life.

It is in the inactive Brahman that one merges, if one seeks Laya or Moksha. One can dwell in the Personal Divine, but one does not merge in him. As for the Supreme Divine he holds in himself the world existence and it is in His consciousness that it moves, so by entering into the Supreme one rises above subjection to Nature, but one does not disappear from all consciousness of world-existence.

The general Divine Will in the universe is for the progressive manifestation in the universe. But that is the general will – it admits the withdrawal of individual souls who are not ready to persevere in the world.

It is not immortality of the body, but the consciousness of immortality *in* the body that can come with the descent of Overmind into Matter or even into the physical mind or with the touch of the modified supramental Light on the physical mind-consciousness. These are preliminary openings, but they are not the supramental fulfilment in Matter.

If the Supramental is decreed, nothing can prevent it; but all things are worked out here through a play of forces, and an unfavourable atmosphere or conditions can delay even when they cannot prevent. Even when a thing is destined, it does not present itself as a certitude in the consciousness here (Overmind-mind-vital-physical) till the play of forces has been worked out up to a certain point at which the descent not only is, but appears as inevitable.

*

How to reconcile:
(1) "Deliver the self by means of the Self." etc. Gita. Chap. VI, 5.
(2) "Abandon all dharmas." etc. Ibid. Chap. XVIII, 66.

There is no real contradiction; the two passages indicate in the Gita's system two different movements of its Yoga, the complete surrender being the crowning movement. One has first to conquer the lower nature, deliver the self involved in the lower movement by means of the higher Self which rises into the divine nature; at the same time one offers all one's actions including the inner action of the Yoga as a sacrifice to the Purushottama, the transcendent and immanent Divine. When one has risen into the higher Self, has the knowledge and is free, one makes the complete surrender to the Divine, abandoning all other dharmas, living only by the divine Consciousness, the divine Will and Force, the divine Ananda.

Our Yoga is not identical with the Yoga of the Gita although it contains all that is essential in the Gita's Yoga. In our Yoga we begin with the idea, the will, the aspiration of the complete surrender; but at the same time we have to reject the lower nature, deliver our consciousness from it, deliver the self involved in the lower nature by the self rising to freedom in the higher nature. If we do not do this double movement, we are in danger of making a tamasic and therefore unreal surrender, making no effort, no tapas and therefore no progress; or else we may make a rajasic surrender not to the Divine but to some self-made false idea or image of the Divine which masks our rajasic ego or something still worse.

*

The spiritual realisation can be had on any plane by contact with the Divine (who is everywhere) or by perception of the Self within, which is pure and untouched by the outer movements. The Supermind is something transcendent – a dynamic Truth-Consciousness which is not there yet, something to be brought down from above.

*

It is not possible to have the direct supramental working now. The Adhar is not yet ready. First one must accept an indirect working which prepares the lower planes for the supramental change.

*

The consciousness which you call supramental is no doubt above the human mind, but it should be called, not the supramental, but simply the higher consciousness. In this higher consciousness there are many degrees, of which the supramental is the summit or the source. It is not possible to reach the summit or source all at once; first of all the lower consciousness has to be purified and made ready. That is the meaning of the Light you saw, whose inner body or substance is too dense and powerful to be penetrated at present.

*

He is using the word supermind too easily. What he describes as supermind is a highly illumined consciousness; a modified supramental light may touch it, but not the full power of Supermind; and, in any case, it is not the Supermind. He speaks of a supramental part which is unreceptive – that is impossible, the supramental cannot be unreceptive. The Supermind is the Truth-Consciousness itself; it already possesses the Truth and does not even need to receive it. The word Vijnana is sometimes used for the higher illumined Intelligence in communication with the Truth, and this must be the part in himself which he felt – but this is not the Supermind. One can enter into Supermind only at the very end of the sadhana, when all difficulties have disappeared and there is no obstacle any longer in the way of the realisation.

*

The universe is certainly or has been up to now in appearance a rough and wasteful game with the dice of chance loaded in favour of the Powers of darkness, the Lords of obscurity, falsehood, death and suffering. But we have to take it as it is and find out – if we reject the way out of the old sages – the way to conquer. Spiritual experience shows that there is behind it all a wide terrain of equality, peace, calm, freedom, and it is only by getting into it that we can have the eye that sees and hope to gain the power that conquers.

*

All that is true Truth is the direct expression in one way or another of the Divine Consciousness. Life is the dynamic expression of Consciousness-Force when thrown outward to realise itself in concrete harmonies of formation; Love is an intense self-expression of the soul of Ananda, and Light is what always accompanies the Supramental Consciousness and its most essential power.

*

It is the supramental Power that transforms mind, life and body – not the Sachchidananda consciousness which supports impartially everything. But it is by having experience of the Sachchidananda, pure existence-consciousness-bliss, that the ascent to the supramental and the descent of the supramental become (at a much later stage) possible. For first one must get free from the ordinary limitation by the mental, vital and physical formations, and the experience of the Sachchidananda peace, calm, purity and wideness gives this liberation.

The Supermind has nothing to do with passing into a blank. It is the Mind overpassing its own limits and following a negative and quietistic way to do it that reaches the big blank. The Mind, being the Ignorance, has to annul itself in order to enter into the supreme Truth – or, at least, so it thinks. But the Supermind being the Truth-Consciousness and the Divine Knowledge has no need to annul itself for the purpose.

*

The supramental change is the ultimate stage of siddhi and it is not likely to come so soon; but there are many levels between the normal mind and the Supermind and it is easy to mistake an ascent into one of them or a descent of their consciousness or influence for a supramental change.

It is quite impossible to ascend to the real Ananda *plane* (except in a profound trance), until after the supramental consciousness has been entered, realised and possessed; but it is quite possible and normal to feel some form of Ananda *consciousness* on any level. This consciousness wherever it is felt is a derivation from the Ananda plane, but it is very much diminished in power and modified to suit the lesser power of receptivity of the inferior levels.

*

The question arose and always arises because of an eagerness in the vital to take any stage of strong experience as the final stage, even to take it for the Overmind, Supermind, full Siddhi. The Supermind or the Overmind either is not so easy to reach as that, even on the side of Knowledge or inner experience only. What you are experiencing belongs to the spiritualised and liberated mind. At this stage there may be intimations from the higher mind levels, but these intimations are merely isolated experiences, not a full change of consciousness. The Supermind is not part of mind or a higher level of mind – it is something entirely different. No sadhak can reach the supermind by his own efforts and the effort to do it by personal tapasya has been the source of many mishaps. One has to go quietly stage by stage until the being is ready and even then it is only the Grace that can bring the real supramental change.

*

The realisation of the Spirit comes long before the development of Overmind or Supermind; hundreds of sadhaks in all times have had the realisation of the Atman in the higher mental planes, *buddheh paratah*, but the supramental realisation was not theirs. One can get partial realisations of the Self or Spirit or the Divine on any plane, mental, vital, physical even, and when one rises above the ordinary mental plane of man into a higher and larger mind, the Self begins to appear in all its conscious wideness.

It is by full entry into this wideness of the Self that cessation of mental activity becomes possible; one gets the inner Silence. After that this inner Silence can remain even when there is activity of any kind; the being remains silent within, the action goes on in the instruments, and one receives all the necessary initiations and execution of action whether mental, vital or physical from a higher source without the fundamental peace and calm of the Spirit being troubled.

The Overmind and Supermind states are something yet higher than this; but before one can understand them, one must first have the self-realisation, the full action of the spiritualised mind and heart, the psychic awakening, the liberation of the imprisoned consciousness, the purification and entire opening of the Adhar. Do not think now of those ultimate things (Overmind, Supermind), but get first these foundations in the liberated nature.

*

This transformation cannot be done individually or in a solitary way only. No individual solitary transformation unconcerned with the work for the earth (which means more than any individual transformation) would be either possible or useful. Also no individual human being can by his own power alone work out the transformation, nor is it the object of the Yoga to create an individual superman here and there. The object of the Yoga is to bring down the supramental consciousness on earth, to fix it there, to create a new race with the principle of the supramental consciousness governing the inner and outer individual and collective life.

That force accepted by individual after individual according to their preparation would establish the supramental consciousness in the physical world and so create a nucleus for its own expansion.

*

It is quite possible that there have been periods of harmony on different levels, not supramental, which were afterwards disturbed – but that could only be a stage or resting place in an arc of spiritual evolution out of the Inconscience.

*

Hostile Forces. The purpose they serve *in the world* is to give a full chance to the possibilities of the Inconscience and Ignorance – for this world was meant to be a working out of these possibilities with the supramental harmonisation as its eventual outcome. The life, the work developing here in the Ashram has to deal with the world problem and has therefore to meet – it could not avoid – the conflict with the working of the hostile Powers in the human being.

*

To speak of "receiving power from the Supramental when we are not conscious" is strange. When one is not conscious, one can still receive a higher force, the Divine Shakti works often from behind the veil, otherwise in the ignorant and unconscious condition of the human being she would not be able to work at all. But the nature of the force or action is modified to suit the condition of the sadhak. One must develop a very full consciousness before one can receive anything from the direct supramental Power and one must be very advanced in consciousness even to receive something of it modified through the Overmind or other intermediate region.

*

This Yoga does not mean a rejection of the powers of life, but an inner transformation and a change of the spirit in the life and the use of the powers. These powers are now used in an egoistic spirit and for undivine ends; they have to be used in a spirit of surrender to the Divine and for the purposes of the divine Work. That is what is meant by conquering them back for the Mother.

*

As for what you write about your experience and your ideas, it looks as if it were simply the old thoughts and movements rising, as they often do, to interfere with the straight course of the sadhana. Mental realisations and ideas of this kind are at best only half-truths and not always even that; once one has taken up a sadhana that goes beyond the mind, it is a mistake to give them too much importance. They can easily become by misapplication a fruitful ground for error.

If you examine the ideas that have come to you, you will see that they are quite inadequate. For example:

1. Matter is *jaḍa* only in appearance. As even modern Science admits, Matter is only energy in action, and, as we know in India, energy is force of consciousness in action.

2. Prakriti in the material world seems to be *jaḍa*, but this too is only an appearance. Prakriti is in reality the conscious power of the Spirit.

3. A bringing down of the Spirit into Matter cannot lead to a *laya* in *jaḍa prakṛti*. A descent of the Spirit could only mean a descent of light, consciousness and power, not a growth of unconsciousness and inertia which is what is meant by the *jaḍa laya*.

4. The Spirit is there already in Matter as everywhere else; it is only a surface apparent unconsciousness or involved consciousness which veils its presence. What we have to do is to awake Matter to the spiritual consciousness concealed in it.

5. What we aim at bringing down into the material world is the supramental consciousness, light and energy, because it is this alone that can truly transform it.

If there is at any time a growth of unconsciousness and inertia, it is because of the resistance of the ordinary nature to the spiritual change. But this is usually raised up in order to be dealt with and eliminated. If it is allowed to remain concealed and not raised up, the difficulty will never be grappled with and no real transformation will take place.

The idea of usefulness to humanity is the old confusion due to secondhand ideas imported from the West. Obviously, to be "useful" to humanity there is no need of Yoga; everyone who leads the human life is useful to humanity in one way or another.

Yoga is directed towards God, not towards man. If a

divine supramental consciousness and power can be brought down and established in the material world, that obviously would mean an immense change for the earth including humanity and its life. But the effect on humanity would only be one result of the change; it cannot be the object of the sadhana. The object of the sadhana can only be to live in the divine consciousness and to manifest it in life.

*

The true object of the Yoga is not philanthropy, but to find the Divine, to enter into the divine consciousness and find one's true being (which is not the ego) in the Divine.

The "Ripus" cannot be conquered by *damana*, (even if it succeeds to some extent, it only keeps them down but does not destroy them); often compression only increases their force. It is only by purification through the Divine Consciousness entering into the egoistic nature and changing it that this thing can be done.

If he gives himself from deep within and is absolutely persevering in the Way, then only can he succeed.

*

This world *is*, as the Gita describes it, *anityamasukham*, so long as we live in the present world-consciousness; it is only by turning from that to the Divine and entering into the Divine Consciousness that one can possess, through the world also, the Eternal.

*

The language of the Gita in many matters seems sometimes contradictory because it admits two apparently opposite truths and tries to reconcile them. It admits the ideal of departure from *saṁsāra* into the Brahman as one possibility; also it affirms the possibility of living free in the Divine (in Me, it says) and acting in the world as the Jivanmukta. It is this latter kind of solution on which it lays the greatest emphasis. So Ramakrishna put the "divine souls" (Ishwarakoti) who can descend the ladder as well as ascend it higher than the Jivas (Jivakoti) who, once having ascended, have not the strength to descend again for divine work. The full truth is in the supramental consciousness and the power to work from there on life and Matter.

*

The Divine can be and is everywhere, masked or half-manifest or beginning to be manifest, in all the planes of consciousness; in the Supramental it begins to be manifest without disguise or veil in its own *svarūpa*.

When the soul is looking from behind, it makes use very often of a very slight coincidence to push the mind and vital into the way.

*

Shiva is the Lord of Tapas. The power is the power of Tapas.

Krishna as a godhead is the Lord of Ananda, Love and Bhakti; as an incarnation, he manifests the union of wisdom (Jnana) and works and leads the earth-evolution through this towards union with the Divine by Ananda, Love and Bhakti.

The Devi is the Divine Shakti – the Consciousness and Power of the Divine, the Mother and Energy of the worlds. All powers are hers. Sometimes Devi-power may mean the power of the universal World-Force; but this is only one side of the Shakti.

PLANES AND PARTS OF THE BEING

Higher Mind is one of the planes of the spiritual mind, the first and lowest of them; it is above the normal mental level. Inner mind is that which lies behind the surface mind (our ordinary mentality) and can only be directly experienced (apart from its vrittis in the surface mind such as philosophy, poetry, idealism, etc.) by sadhana, by breaking down the habit of being on the surface and by going deeper within.

Larger mind is a general term to cover the realms of mind which become our field whether by going within or widening into the cosmic consciousness.

The true mental being is not the same as the inner mental – true mental, true vital, true physical being means the Purusha of that level freed from the error and ignorant thought and will of the lower Prakriti and directly open to the knowledge and guidance above.

Higher vital usually refers to the vital mind and emotive being as opposed to the middle vital which has its seat in the navel and is dynamic, sensational and passionate and the lower which is made up of the smaller movements of human life-desire and life-reactions.

*

The mind proper is divided into three parts – thinking Mind, dynamic Mind, externalising Mind – the former concerned with ideas and knowledge in their own right, the second with the putting out of mental forces or realisation of the idea, the third with the expression of them in life (not only by speech, but by any form it can give). The word "physical mind" is rather ambiguous, because it can mean this externalising Mind and the mental in the physical taken together.

Vital Mind proper is a sort of a mediator between vital emotion, desire, impulsion, etc. and the mental proper. It expresses the desires, feelings, emotions, passions, ambitions, possessive and active tendencies of the vital and throws them into mental forms (the pure imaginations or dreams of greatness, happiness, etc. in which men indulge are one peculiar form of the vital-mind activity). There is still a lower stage of the mental in the vital which merely expresses the vital stuff without subjecting it to any play of intelligence. It is through this mental vital that the vital passions, impulses, desires rise up and get into the Buddhi and either cloud or distort it.

As the vital Mind is limited by the vital view and feeling of things (while the dynamic Intelligence is not, for it acts by the idea and reason), so the mind in the physical or mental physical is limited by the physical view and experience of things, it mentalises the experiences brought by the physical view and experience of things, and does not go beyond that (though it can do that much very cleverly), unlike the externalising mind which deals with them more from the reason and its higher intelligence. But in practice these two usually get mixed together. The mechanical mind is a much lower action of the mental physical which, left to itself, would only repeat customary ideas and record the natural reflexes of the physical consciousness to the contacts of outward life and things.

The lower vital as distinguished from the higher is concerned only with the small greeds, small desires, small passions, etc. which make up the daily stuff of life for the ordinary sensational man – while the vital-physical proper is the nervous being giving vital reflexes to contacts of things with the physical consciousness.

*

Most men are, like animals, driven by the forces of Nature: whatever desires come, they fulfil them, whatever emotions come they allow them to play, whatever physical wants they have, they try to satisfy. We say then that the activities and feelings of men are controlled by their Prakriti, and mostly by the vital and physical nature. The body is the instrument of the Prakriti or Nature – it obeys its own nature or it obeys the vital forces of desire, passion, etc.

But man has also a mind and, as he develops, he learns to control his vital and physical nature by his reason and by his will. This control is very partial: for the reason is often deluded by vital desires and the ignorance of the physical and it puts itself on their side and tries to justify by its ideas, reasonings or arguments their mistakes and wrong movements. Even if the reason keeps free and tells the vital or the body, "Do not do this", yet the vital and the body often follow their own movement in spite of the prohibition – man's mental will is not strong enough to compel them.

When people do sadhana, there is a higher Nature that works within, the psychic and spiritual, and they have to put their nature under the influence of the psychic being and the higher spiritual self or of the Divine. Not only the vital and the body but the mind also has to learn the Divine Truth and obey the divine rule. But because of the lower nature and its continued hold on them, they are unable at first and for a long time to prevent their nature from following the old ways – even when they know or are told from within what to do or what not to do. It is only by persistent sadhana, by getting into the higher spiritual consciousness and spiritual nature that this difficulty can be overcome; but even for the strongest and best sadhaks it takes a long time.

*

The heart is the centre of the emotional being, the highest part of the vital. The navel is the centre of the dynamic and sensational vital. The centre below the navel and the Muladhar commands the lower vital (physical desires, small greeds, passions, etc.). The throat centre is not the vital – it is the physical mind, the expressive externalising consciousness. What you feel may be the vital taking hold of the physical mind and moving it for expression (this is the source of pride, sense of possession, ambition, anger and other passions) – but it expresses them often enough through the heart centre.

*

The inner being is the inner mind, inner vital, inner physical with the psychic behind them. The phrase 'higher being' is used to denote the conscious self on the planes higher than the ordinary human consciousness.

*

The psychic has the position you speak of, because the psychic is in touch with the Divine in the lower nature. But the inner mind, vital and physical are a part of the universal and open to the dualities – only they are wider than the external mind, life and body, and can receive more largely and easily the divine influence.

*

Our inner being is in touch with universal mind, life and Matter; it is a part of all that, but by that very fact it cannot be in possession of liberation and peace. You are thinking probably of the Atman and confusing it with the inner being.

*

In the navel is the main seat of the dynamic vital consciousness whose range is from the heart level to the centre below the navel (lower vital, sensational desire centre). These three mark the domain of the vital being. The centre of the psychic is behind the heart and it is through the purified emotions that the psychic most easily finds an outlet. All from the heart above is the domain of the mental being – with also three centres, one in the throat (the outward-going or externalising mind), one between the eyes or rather in the middle of the forehead (the centre of vision and will) and one above communicating with the brain which is called the thousand-petalled lotus and where are centralised the thinking mind and higher intelligence communicating with the greater mind planes (illumined mind, intuition, overmind) above.

In the outer surface nature mind, psychic, vital, physical are jumbled together and it needs a strong power of introspection, self-analysis, close observation and disentanglement of the threads of thought, feeling and impulse to find out the composition of our nature and the relation and interaction of these parts upon each other. But when we go inside, we find the sources of all this surface action and there the parts of our being are quite clearly distinct from each other; it is as if we were a group-being, each member of the group with its separate place and function, and all directed by a central being who is sometimes in front above the others, sometimes behind the scenes.

*

The soul and the life are two quite different powers. The soul is a spark of the Divine Spirit which supports the individual nature; mind, life, body are the instruments for the manifestation of the nature. In most men the soul is hidden and covered over by the action of the external nature; they mistake the vital being for the soul, because it is the vital which animates and moves the body. But this vital being is a thing made up of desires and executive forces, good and bad; it is the desire-soul, not the true thing. It is when the true soul (psyche) comes forward and begins first to influence and then govern the actions of the instrumental nature that man begins to overcome vital desire and grow towards a divine nature.

*

The centres or Chakras are seven in number:–
    (1) The thousand-petalled lotus on the top of the head.
    (2) In the middle of the forehead – the Ajna Chakra – (will, vision, dynamic thought).
    (3) Throat centre – externalising mind.
    (4) Heart-lotus – emotional centre. The psychic is behind it.

(5) Navel – higher vital (proper).
(6) Below navel – lower vital.
(7) Muladhara – physical.

All these centres are in the middle of the body; they are supposed to be attached to the spinal chord; but in fact all these things are in the subtle body, *sūkṣma deha*, though one has the feeling of their activities as if in the physical body when the consciousness is awake.

*

You are reasoning on the analogy of our own very cabined and limited sense-consciousness and its rather clumsy relations with the happenings in material space. What is space after all but an extension of conscious being in which Consciousness-Force builds its own surroundings? In the subtle physical plane there are, not one, but many layers of consciousness and each moves in its own being, that is to say, in its own space. I have said that each subtle plane is a conglomeration or series of worlds. Each space may at any point meet, penetrate or coincide with another; accordingly at one point of meeting or coincidence there might be several subtle objects occupying what we might rather arbitrarily call the same space, and yet they may not be in any actual relation with each other. If there is a relation created, it is the multiple consciousness of the seer in which the meeting-place becomes apparent that creates it.

On the other hand, there may be a relation between objects in different regions of space correlated to each other as in the case of the gross physical object and its subtle counterpart. There you can more easily reason of relations between one space and another.

*

Patala is evidently here a name for the subconscient – the beings there have "no heads", that is to say, there is there no mental consciousness; men have all of them such a subconscient plane in their own being and from there rise all sorts of irrational and ignorant (headless) instincts, impulsions, memories, etc., which have an effect upon their acts and feelings without their detecting the real source. At night many incoherent dreams come from this world or plane. The world above is the superconscient plane of being – above the human consciousness – there are many worlds of that kind; these are divine worlds.

*

The individual is not limited to the physical body – it is only the external consciousness which feels like that. As soon as one gets over this feeling of limitation one can feel first the inner consciousness which is connected with the body, but does not belong to it, afterwards the planes of consciousness surrounding the body, but part of oneself, part of the individual being, through which one is in contact with the cosmic forces and also with other beings. This last is the environmental consciousness.

*

The centre of vision is between the eyebrows in the centre of the forehead. When it opens one gets the inner vision, sees the inner forms and images of things and people and begins to understand things and people from within and not only from outside, develops a power of will which also acts in the inner (Yogic) way on things and people etc.

Its opening is often the beginning of the Yogic as opposed
to the ordinary mental consciousness.

*

I never heard of two lotuses in the heart centre; but it is
the seat of two powers, in front the higher vital or emotional being, behind and concealed the soul or psychic
being.

The colours of the lotuses and the numbers of petals are
respectively, from bottom to top: – (1) the Muladhara or
physical consciousness centre, four petals, red; (2) the
abdominal centre, six petals, deep purple red; (3) the navel
centre, ten petals, violet; (4) the heart centre, twelve
petals, golden pink; (5) the throat centre, sixteen petals,
grey; (6) the forehead centre between the eyebrows, two
petals, white; (7) the thousand-petalled lotus above the
head, blue with gold light around. The functions are,
according to our Yoga, – (1) commanding the physical
consciousness and the subconscient; (2) commanding the
small vital movements, the little greeds, lusts, desires, the
small sense-movements; (3) commanding the larger life-
forces and the passions and larger desire-movements; (4)
commanding the higher emotional being with the psychic
deep behind it; (5) commanding expression and all exter-
nalisation of the mind movements and mental forces; (6)
commanding thought, will, vision; (7) commanding the
higher thinking mind and the illumined mind and opening
upwards to the intuition and overmind. The seventh is
sometimes or by some identified with the brain, but that is
an error – the brain is only a channel of communication
situated between the thousand-petalled and the forehead
centre. The former is sometimes called the void centre,

śunya, either because it is not in the body, but in the apparent void above or because rising above the head one enters first into the silence of the self or spiritual being.

*

A strong vital is one that is full of life-force, has ambition, courage, great energy, a force for action or creation, a large expansive movement whether for generosity in giving or for possession and lead and domination, a power to fulfil and materialise – many other forms of vital strength are there also. It is often difficult for such a vital to surrender itself because of the sense of its own powers – but if it can do so, it becomes an admirable instrument for the Divine Work.

*

No, a weak vital has not the strength to turn spiritually – and being weak, more easily falls under a wrong influence and even when it wants, finds it difficult to accept anything beyond its own habitual nature. The strong vital, when the will is there, can do it much more easily – its own central difficulty is the pride of the ego and the attraction of its powers.

The chest has more connection with the psychic than the vital. A strong vital may have a good physical, but as often it has not – it draws too much on the physical, eats it up as it were.

CONDITIONS FOR SADHANA

Openness and, whenever needed, passivity, but to the highest consciousness, not to anything that comes.

Therefore, there must be a certain quiet vigilance even in the passivity. Otherwise there may be either wrong movements or inertia.

*

Your former sadhana was mostly on the vital plane. The experiences of the vital plane are very interesting to the sadhak but they are mixed, i.e., not all linked with the higher Truth. A greater, purer and firmer basis for the sadhana has to be established – the psychic basis. For that reason all the old experiences are stopped. The heart has to be made the centre and through bhakti and aspiration you have to bring forward the psychic being and enter into close touch with the Divine Shakti. If you can do this, your sadhana will begin again with a better result.

*

When the light and peace are full in the vital and physical consciousness, it is this that remains always as a basis for the right movement of the whole nature.

To remain within, above and untouched, full of the inner consciousness and the inner experience, – listening when need be to one or another with the surface consciousness, but with even that undisturbed, not either pulled outwards or invaded, that is the perfect condition for the sadhana.

*

The Mother's help is always there for those who are willing to receive it. But you must be conscious of your vital nature, and the vital nature must consent to change. It is no use merely observing that it is unwilling and that, when thwarted, it creates depression in you. Always the vital nature is not at first willing and always when it is thwarted or asked to change, it creates this depression by its revolt or refusal of consent. You have to insist till it recognises the truth and is willing to be transformed and to accept the Mother's help and grace. If the mind is sincere and the psychic aspiration complete and true, the vital can always be made to change.

*

To read what will help the Yoga or what will be useful for the work or what will develop the capacities for the divine purpose. Not to read worthless stuff or for mere entertainment or for a dilettante intellectual curiosity which is of the nature of a mental dram-drinking. When one is established in the highest consciousness, one can read nothing or everything; it makes no difference – but that is still far off.

*

I see no objection to his going on with his studies, – whether they will be of any use to him for a life of sadhana will depend on the spirit in which he does them. The really important thing is to develop a state of consciousness in which one can live in the Divine and act from it on the physical world. A mental training and discipline, knowledge of men and things, culture, capacities of a useful kind are a preparation that the sadhak would be all the better for having – even though they are not the one thing indispensable. Education in India gives very little of these things, but if one knows how to study without caring much for the form or for mere academic success, the life of the student can be used for the purpose.

*

Every artist almost (there are rare exceptions) has got something of the "public" man in him, in his vital-physical parts, the need of the stimulus of an audience, social applause, satisfied vanity or fame. That must go absolutely, if he wants to be a Yogi and his art a service not of man or of his own ego but of the Divine.

*

In the most physical things you have to fix a programme in order to deal with them, otherwise all becomes a sea of confusion and haphazard. Fixed rules have also to be made for the management of material things so long as people are not sufficiently developed to deal with them in the right way without rules. But in matters of the inner development and the sadhana it is impossible to map out a plan fixed in every detail and say, "Every time you shall stop here, there, in this way, on that line and no other." Things would become so tied up and rigid that nothing could be done; there could be no true and effective movement.

Everything depends on the inner condition and the outward condition is only useful as a means and a help for expressing or confirming the inner condition and making it dynamic and effective. If you do or say a thing with the psychic uppermost or with the right inner touch, it will be effective; if you do or say the same thing out of the mind or the vital or with a wrong or mixed atmosphere, it may be quite ineffective. To do the right thing in the right way in each case and at each moment one must be in the right consciousness – it cannot be done by following a fixed mental rule which under some circumstances might fit in and under others might not fit at all. A general principle can be laid down if it is in consonance with the Truth, but its application must be determined by the inner consciousness seeing at each step what is to be done and not done. If the psychic is uppermost, if the being is entirely turned towards the Mother and follows the psychic, this can be increasingly done.

*

It is true that one has to try to keep the inner condition under all circumstances, even the most adverse; but that does not mean one has to accept, unnecessarily, unfavourable conditions when there is no good reason for their being allowed to go on. Especially, the nervous system and the physical cannot bear an excessive strain, – the mind too and the higher vital; your fatigue came from the strain of living in One Consciousness and at the same time exposing yourself too much to prolonged contacts from the ordinary consciousness. A certain amount of self-defence is necessary, so that the consciousness may not be pulled down or out constantly into the ordinary atmosphere or the physical strained by being forced into activities that have become foreign to you. Those who practise Yoga often seek refuge in solitude from these difficulties; that is unnecessary here, but all the same you need not submit to being put under this kind of useless strain always.

*

Wanton waste, careless spoiling of physical things in an incredibly short time, loose disorder, misuse of service and materials due either to vital grasping or to tamasic inertia are baneful to prosperity and tend to drive away or discourage the Wealth-Power. These things have long been rampant in the society and, if that continues, an increase in our means might well mean proportionate increase in the wastage and disorder and neutralise the material advantage. This must be remedied if there is to be any sound progress.

Asceticism for its own sake is not the ideal of this Yoga, but self-control in the vital and right order in the material are very important part of it – and an ascetic discipline is better than loose absence of true control. Mastery of the material does not mean having plenty and profusely throwing it out or spoiling it as fast as it comes or faster. Mastery implies the right and careful utilisation of things and also a self-control in their use.

*

The best way to prepare oneself for the spiritual life when one has to live in the ordinary occupations and surroundings is to cultivate an entire equality and detachment and the *samatā* of the Gita with the faith that the Divine is there and the Divine Will at work in all things even though at present under the conditions of a world of Ignorance. Beyond this the Light and Ananda towards which life is working, but the best way for the advent and foundation in the individual being and nature is to grow in this spiritual equality. That would also solve your difficulty about things unpleasant and disagreeable. All unpleasantness should be faced with this spirit of *samatā*.

To remain open to the Mother is to remain always quiet
and happy and confident – not restless, not grieving or
despondent, to let her force work in you, guide you, give
you knowledge, give you peace and Ananda. If you cannot
keep yourself open, then aspire constantly but quietly that
you may be open.

*

You are the Mother's child and the Mother's love to her
children is without limit and she bears patiently with the
defects of their nature. Try to be the true child of the
Mother: it is there within you, but your outward mind is
occupied by little futile things and too often in a violent fuss
over them. You must not only see the Mother in dream but
learn to see and feel her with you and within you at all
times. Then you would find it easier to control yourself and
change, – for she being there would be able to do it for you.

*

The psychic self-control that is desirable in these surroundings and in the midst of discussion would mean
among other things:

(1) Not to allow the impulse of speech to assert itself too
much or say anything without reflection, but to speak
always with a conscious control and only what is necessary
and helpful.

(2) To avoid all debate, dispute or too animated discussion and simply say what has to be said and leave it
there. There should also be no insistence that you are right
and the others wrong, but what is said should only be
thrown in as a contribution to the consideration of the truth
of the matter.

(3) To keep the tone of speech and the wording very quiet and calm and uninsistent.

(4) Not to mind at all if others are heated and dispute, but remain quiet and undisturbed and yourself speak only what can help things to be smooth again.

(5) If there is gossip about others and harsh criticism (especially about sadhaks), not to join – for these things are helpful in no way and only lower the consciousness from its higher level.

(6) To avoid all that would hurt or wound others.

*

How are you going to find the right external relations by withdrawing altogether from external relations? And how do you propose to be thoroughly transformed and unified by living only in the internal life, without any test of the transformation and unity by external contact and the ordeals of the external work and life? Thoroughness includes external work and relations and not a retired inner life only.

It is only by the vital ego giving up its demands and claims and the reactions these produce when not satisfied, that the transformation and unification can come, and there is no other way.

*

The attitude which he describes, if he keeps it correctly, is the right one. It brought him at first the beginning of a true experience, the Light (white and golden) and the Force pouring down from the Sahasradal and filling the system; but when it touched the vital parts it must have awakened the prana energies in the vital centres (navel and below) and as these were not pure, all the impurities arose (anger, sex, fear, doubt, etc.) and the mind became clouded by the uprush of impure vital forces. He says that all this is now subsiding, the mind is becoming calm and in the vital the impulses come but do not remain. Not only the mind but the vital must become calm; these impulses must lose their force of recurrence by rejection and purification. Entire purity and peace must be established in the whole Adhar; it is only then that he will have a safe and sure basis for further progress.

The reason why the force flows out of him must be because he allows himself to become too inertly passive and open to everything. One must be passive only to the Divine Force, but vigilant not to put oneself at the mercy of all forces. If he becomes passive when he tries to see God in another person, he is likely to put himself at the disposal of any force that is working through that person and his own forces may be drained away towards the other. It is better for him not to try in this way; let him aspire for the Peace and Strength that come from above and for entire purity and open himself to that Force only. Such experiences as the feeling of the Divine everywhere (not in this or that person only) will then come of themselves.

Our object is the supramental realisation and we have to do whatever is necessary for that or towards that under the conditions of each stage. At present the necessity is to prepare the physical consciousness; for that a complete equality and peace and a complete dedication free from personal demand or desire in the physical and the lower vital parts is the thing to be established. Other things can come in their proper time. What is the need now is not insistence on physical nearness, which is one of these other

things, but the psychic opening in the physical consciousness and the constant presence and guidance there.

*

There should be no straining after power, no ambition,
no egoism of power. The power or powers that come
should be considered not as one's own, but as gifts of the
Divine for the Divine's purpose. Care should be taken that
there should be no ambitious or selfish misuse, no pride or
vanity, no sense of superiority, no claim or egoism of the
instrument, only a simple and pure psychic instrumentation
of the nature in any way in which it is fit for the service of
the Divine.

*

You can certainly go on developing the consciousness of
the Witness Purusha above, but if it is only a witness and
the lower Prakriti is allowed to have its own way, there
would be no reason why it should ever stop. Many take that
attitude – that the Purusha has to liberate itself by standing
apart, and the Prakriti can be allowed to go on till the end of
the life doing its own business – it is *prārabdha karma*;
when the body falls away, the Prakriti will drop also and the
Purusha go off into the featureless Brahman! This is a
comfortable theory, but of more than doubtful truth; I
don't think liberation is so simple and facile a matter as
that. In any case, the transformation which is the object of
our Yoga would not take place.

The Purusha above is not only a Witness, he is the giver
(or withholder) of the sanction; if he persistently refuses
the sanction to a movement of Prakriti, keeping himself

detached, then, even if it goes on for a time by its past momentum, it usually loses its hold after a time, becomes more feeble, less persistent, less concrete and in the end fades away. If you take the Purusha consciousness, it should be not only as the Witness but as the Anumanta, refusing sanction to the disturbing movements, sanctioning only peace, calm, purity and whatever else is part·of the divine nature. This refusal of sanction need not mean a struggle with the lower Prakriti; it should be a quiet, persistent, detached refusal leaving unsupported, unassented to, without meaning or justification, the contrary action of the nature.

Never consent to the ideas, suggestions, feelings that bring back the cloud, the confusion and the revolt. It is the consent that makes these strong to recur. Refuse the consent and they will be obliged to retire either immediately or after a time.

Remain fixed in the sunlight of the true consciousness – for only there is happiness and peace. They do not depend upon outside happenings, but on this alone.

*

Take with you the peace and quietude and joy and keep it by remembering always the Divine.

If the thoughts about the past and the future come merely as memories and imaginations, they are of no use and you should quietly turn away your mind from them back to the Divine and to the Yoga. If they are anything to the purpose, then refer them to the Divine, put them in the light of the Truth, so that you may have the truth about them or the right decision or formation for the future, if any decision is needed.

There is no harm in the tears of which you speak, they come from the soul, the psychic being, and are a help and not a hindrance.

*

A mere restless dissatisfaction with the ordinary life is not a sufficient preparation for this Yoga. A positive inner call, a strong will and a great steadiness are necessary for success in the spiritual life.

*

The Mother does not discuss these mental problems with the disciples. It is quite useless trying to reconcile these things with the intellect. For there are two things, the Ignorance from which the struggle and discord come and the secret Light, Unity, Bliss and Harmony. The intellect belongs to the Ignorance. It is only by getting into a better consciousness that one can live in the Light and Bliss and Unity and not be touched by the outward discord and struggle. That change of consciousness therefore is the only thing that matters, to reconcile with the intellect would make no difference.

*

The constant presence of the Mother comes by practice; the Divine Grace is essential for success in the sadhana, but it is the practice that prepares the descent of the Grace.

You have to learn to go inward, ceasing to live in external things only, quiet the mind and aspire to become aware of the Mother's workings in you.

*

If he wants to make himself some day fit for the spiritual life, the first thing to be avoided is vital restlessness. To do the work one has to do with a quiet mind, making an offering of it to the Divine and trying to get rid of egoism and vital desire, is the best way to prepare oneself.

*

Live always as if you were under the very eye of the Supreme and of the Divine Mother. Do nothing, try to think and feel nothing that would be unworthy of the Divine Presence.

*

The Presence whose fading you regret can only be felt if the inner being continues to be consecrated and the outer nature is put into harmony or at least kept under the touch of the inner spirit. But if you do things which your inner being does not approve, this condition will be eventually tarnished and, each time, the possibility of your feeling the Presence will diminish. You must have a strong will to purification and an aspiration that does not flag and cease, if the Mother's grace is to be there and effective.

*

All I can suggest to him is to practise some kind of Karmayoga – remembering the Supreme in all his actions from the smallest to the greatest, doing them with a quiet mind and without ego-sense or attachment and offering them to Him as a sacrifice. He may also try or aspire to feel the presence of the Divine Shakti behind the world and its forces, distinguish between the lower nature of the Ignorance and the higher divine nature whose character is absolute calm, peace, power, Light and Bliss and aspire to be raised and led gradually from the lower to the higher.

If he can do this, he will become fit in time to dedicate himself to the Divine and lead a wholly spiritual life.

*

It is necessary if you want to progress in your sadhana that you should make the submission and surrender of which you speak sincere, real and complete. This cannot be as long as you mix up your desires with your spiritual aspiration. It cannot be as long as you cherish vital attachment to family, child or anything or anybody else. If you are to do this Yoga, you must have only one desire and aspiration, to receive the spiritual Truth and manifest it in all your thoughts, feelings, actions and nature. You must not hunger after any relations with anyone. The relations of the sadhak with others must be created for him from within, and when he has the true consciousness and lives in the Light. They will be determined within him by the power and will of the Divine Mother according to the supramental Truth for the divine life and the divine work; they must not be determined by his mind and his vital desires. This is the thing you have to remember. Your psychic being is capable of giving itself to the Mother and living and growing in the Truth; but your lower vital being has been full of attachments and *saṁskāras* and an impure movement of desire and your external physical mind was not able to shake off its ignorant ideas and habits and open to the Truth. That was the reason why you were unable to progress, because you were keeping up an element and movements which could not be allowed to remain; for they were the exact opposite of what has to be established in a divine life. The Mother can only free you from these things, if you really want it, not only in your psychic being, but in your physical mind and all your vital nature. The sign will be that you no longer cherish or insist on your personal notions, attachments or desires, and that whatever the distance or wherever you may be, you will feel yourself open and the power and presence of the Mother with you and working in you and will be contented, quiet, confident, wanting nothing else, awaiting always the Mother's will.

*

If your faith is getting firmer day by day, you are certainly progressing in your sadhana and there can have been no fall. An interruption of definite experiences may be only a period of assimilation in which one prepares for a new range of experience. Keep yourself open and aspire.

*

Those who fall into insanity have lost the true touch and got into the wrong contact. It is due either to some impurity and unspiritual desire with which the seeker enters into the way or some insincerity, egoism and false attitude or to some weakness in the brain or nervous system which cannot bear the Power it has called down into it.

The safest way is to follow the guidance of someone who has himself attained to mastery in the path. Only that guidance should be implicitly and sincerely followed; one's own mind and its ideas and fancies must not be allowed to interfere. It goes without saying that it must be a true guidance, not the leading of a tyro or an imposter.

*

This state which tries to come upon you and seize is not part of your true self, but a foreign influence. To yield to it and to express it would therefore be not sincerity, but the expression of something false to your true being, something that will grow more and more foreign to you as you progress. Always reject it, when it comes, even if you feel strongly its touch; open in your mind and soul to the Mother, keep your will and faith and you will find it receding. Even if it returns obstinately, be equally and more obstinate against it, firm in rejection – that will discourage and wear it out and finally it will grow weak, a shadow of itself and disappear.

Be true to your true self always – that is the real sincerity. Persist and conquer.

I think you have always had an idea that to give expression to an impulse or a movement is the best way or even the only way to get rid of it. But that is a mistaken idea. If you give expression to anger, you prolong or confirm the habit of the recurrence of anger; you do not diminish or get rid of the habit. The very first step towards weakening the power of anger in the nature and afterwards getting rid of it altogether is to refuse all expression to it in act or speech. Afterwards one can go on with more likelihood of success to throw it out from the thought and feeling also. And so with all other wrong movements.

All these movements come from outside, from the universal lower Nature or are suggested or thrown upon you by adverse forces – adverse to your spiritual progress. Your method of taking them as your own is again a wrong method; for by doing that you increase their power to recur and take hold of you. If you take them as your own, that gives them a kind of right to be there. If you feel them as *not* your own, then they have no right, and the will can develop more power to send them away. What you must always have and feel as yours is this will, the power to refuse assent, to refuse admission to a wrong movement. Or if it comes in, the power to send it away, without expressing it.

Of course the best way will be if you can keep the contact more with the Mother and her Light and Force and receive and accept and follow only what comes from that higher force.

*

It is not Yoga to give free play to the natural instincts and desires. Yoga demands mastery over the nature, not subjection to the nature.

*

The only way to get rid of these vital movements is to do persistently what he describes himself as doing with the invading forces – i.e. he must be always vigilant, try always at every moment to be conscious, always reject these things, refusing to take pleasure in them, call on the Mother, bring down the descent of the Light. If they return persistently he must not be discouraged; it is not possible to change the nature at once, it takes a long time. If, however, he can keep the psychic consciousness in the front, then it will be much easier and there will be much less difficulty and trouble in the change. That can be done by constant aspiration and *abhyāsa*.

*

It is difficult for the ordinary Christian to be of a piece, because the teachings of Christ are on quite another plane from the consciousness of the intellectual and vital man trained by the education and society of Europe – the latter, even as a minister or priest, has never been called upon to practise what he preached in entire earnest. But it is difficult for the human nature anywhere to think, feel and act from one centre of true faith, belief or vision. The average Hindu considers the spiritual life the highest, reveres the Sannyasi, is moved by the Bhakta; but if one of the family circle leaves the world for spiritual life, what tears, arguments, remonstrances, lamentations! It is almost worse than if he had died a natural death. It is not conscious mental insincerity – they will argue like Pandits and go to Shastra to prove you in the wrong; it is unconsciousness, a vital insincerity which they are not aware of and which uses the reasoning mind as an accomplice.

That is why we insist so much on sincerity in the Yoga – and that means to have all the being consciously turned towards the one Truth, the one Divine. But that for human nature is one of the most difficult of tasks, much more difficult than a less rigid asceticism or a fervent piety. Religion itself does not give this complete harmonised sincerity – it is only the psychic being and the one-souled spiritual aspiration that can give it.

*

A human vital interchange cannot be a true support for the sadhana and is, on the contrary, sure to impair and distort it, leading to self-deception in the consciousness and a wrong turn of the emotional being and vital nature.

*

If you want to change, you must first resolutely get rid of the defects of your vital being, persevering steadily, however difficult it may be or however long it may take, calling in always the divine help and compelling yourself always to be entirely sincere.

As for fitness and unfitness, nobody is entirely fit for this Yoga; one has to become fit by aspiration, by *abhyāsa*, by sincerity and surrender. If you have always desired the spiritual life, it is the psychic part of you that desired it, but your vital has always come in the way. Establish a sincere will in the vital; do not allow personal desires and demands and selfishness and falsehood to mix in your sadhana; then alone the vital in you will become fit for the sadhana.

If you want your endeavour to succeed, it must become always purer and more steady and persistent. If you practise sincerely, you will get the help needed by you.

*

It is the past habit of the vital that makes you repeatedly go out into the external part; you must persist and establish the opposite habit of living in your inner being which is your true being and of looking at everything from there. It is from there that you get the true thought, the true vision and understanding of things and of your own self and nature.

*

It is always the habit of the vital being to find out things by which it persuades the mind and justifies its desires; and circumstances usually shape themselves to justify it still further. For what we have within us creates the circumstances outside us. What matters is that you should take inwardly a different position in the future.

*

Concentration in the heart is best aided if possible by the power and light descending from above the head.

Do not yield to the Tamas; the more you yield, the more it will stick.

For all these things, the way is detachment, to stand back; separate yourself from the desire, observe it, refuse sanction and put a quiet and persistent will for it to cease, calling on the Mother's force at the same time to dissolve and eliminate the greed, desire, attachment, obscurity or inertia. If sincerely, persistently and rightly done, it will succeed in the end, even though it may take time.

*

The relation of Guru and disciple is only one of many relations which one can have with the Divine, and in this Yoga which aims at a supramental realisation, it is not usual to give it this name; rather, the Divine is regarded as the Source, the living Sun of Light and Knowledge and Consciousness and spiritual realisation; all that one receives is felt as coming from there and the whole being remoulded by the Divine Hand. This is a greater and more intimate relation than that of the human Guru and disciple, which is more of a limited mental ideal. Nevertheless, if the mind still needs the more familiar mental conception, it can be kept so long as it is needed; only do not let the soul be bound by it and do not let it limit the inflow of other relations with the Divine and larger forms of experience.

*

You have apparently a call and may be fit for Yoga; but there are different paths and each has a different aim and end before it. It is common to all the paths to conquer the desires, to put aside the ordinary relations of life, and to try to pass from uncertainty to everlasting certitude. One may also try to conquer dream and sleep, thirst and hunger etc. But it is no part of my Yoga to have nothing to do with the world or with life or to kill the senses or entirely inhibit their action. It is the object of my Yoga to transform life by bringing down into it the Light, Power and Bliss of the divine Truth and its dynamic certitudes. This Yoga is not a Yoga of world-shunning asceticism, but of divine life. Your object on the other hand can only be gained by entering into Samadhi and ceasing in it from all connection with world-existence.

*

In the way of meditating of which we spoke, aspiration, prayer, concentration, intensity are a natural part of it. Those who take it go quicker and develop their sadhana, once they get fixed in it, much more easily as well as smoothly than by a distressed, doubtful and anxious straining with revulsions of despondency and turning away from hope and endeavour. We spoke of a steady opening to the Divine with a flow of the force doing its work in the Adhar, a poised opening with a quiet mind and heart full of trust and the sunlight of confidence; where do you find that we said a helpless waiting must be your programme?

As for light-heartedness and insouciance – a light don't-care attitude is the last thing we would recommend to anybody. The Mother spoke of cheerfulness, and if she used the word light-hearted, it was not in the sense of anything lightly or frivolously gay and careless – although a deeper and finer gaiety can have its place as an element of the Yogic character. What she meant was a glad equanimity even in the face of difficulties and there is nothing in that contrary to Yogic teaching or to her own practice. The vital nature on the surface (the depths of the true vital are different) is attached on the one side to a superficial mirth and enjoyment, on the other to sorrow and despair and gloom and tragedy, – for these are for it the cherished lights and shades of life; but a bright or wide and free peace or an *ānandamaya* intensity or, best, a fusing of both in one is the true poise of both the soul and the mind – and of the true vital also – in Yoga. It is perfectly possible for a quite human sadhak to get to such a poise, it is not necessary to be divine before one can attain it.

It is quite true that rising into a higher consciousness than the ordinary human consciousness is the right way towards transformation. Merely to remain in the ordinary lower consciousness and try to reject from there the wrong movements can produce no permanent or complete result. But there are several points here which you must note or this perception may be accompanied by an error.

(1) As you have yourself subsequently seen, all the parts and personalities that constitute the being must share in the higher consciousness, otherwise the old movements under various pretexts will continue.

(2) You speak of rejecting the lower vital, but it is only the unregenerated lower vital movements that can be got rid of; you cannot get rid of the lower vital itself, for it is a necessary part of the manifested nature, like the higher vital or the mind. It has to be changed in the power of the higher consciousness, not left to itself or dropped from you.

(3) If you do not so change it, if you simply remain

content by living in the psychic or other higher consciousness internally, then you run the risk of doing like those
who are satisfied to have experiences and some inner
quietude or Ananda, but leave the external nature and
surface active movements unchanged, either thinking them
of no importance or justifying them under the plea that
there is the psychic or spiritual consciousness behind them.

*

It is a mistake to think that by fearing or being unhappy
you can progress. Fear is always a feeling to be rejected,
because what you fear is just the thing that is likely to
come to you: fear attracts the object of fear. Unhappiness
weakens the strength and lays one more open to the causes
of unhappiness.

One can be quiet, happy, cheerful without being all that
in a light or shallow way – and the happiness need not bring
any vital reaction. All that you need to do is to be observant
and vigilant, – watchful so that you may not give assent to
wrong movements or the return of the old feelings, darkness, confusion, etc. If you remain vigilant, then with the
increase of the Force upholding you, a power of self-
control will come, a power to see and reject the wrong turn
or the wrong reaction when it comes. Fear and unhappiness
will not give you that. It is only by this vigilance accompanied by an opening to the supporting and guiding Force
that it will come. What you describe as a capacity to choose
the right and the feeling of strength or power that can stop
the wrong movement and take the right one as soon as it
recognises them is just this control and vigilance. It is by
this control and vigilance supported by the Force that you
can prevent the love and devotion too from being mixed

with or replaced by selfish desires and impurities. The more you open, the more this power will increase in you.

*

Up to now no liberated man has objected to the Guru-vada; it is usually only people who live in the mind or vital and have the pride of the mind and the arrogance of the vital that find it below their dignity to recognise a Guru.

*

To give up restraint would be to give free play to the vital and that would mean leave for all kinds of forces to enter in. So long as there is not the supramental consciousness controlling and penetrating everything, in all the being from the overmind downwards, there is an ambiguous play of forces, and each force, however divine in origin, may be used by the Powers of light or intercepted as it passes through the mind and the vital by the Powers of darkness. Vigilance, discrimination, control cannot be abandoned till the complete victory has been won and the consciousness transmuted.

BASES OF SADHANA

It is because your consciousness in the course of the sadhana has come into contact with the lower physical nature and sees it as it is in itself when it is not kept down or controlled either by the mind, the psychic or the spiritual force. This nature is in itself full of low and obscure desires, it is the most animal part of the human being. One has to come into contact with it so as to know what is there and transform it. Most sadhaks of the old type are satisfied with rising into the spiritual or psychic realms and leave this part to itself – but by that it remains unchanged, even if mostly quiescent, and no complete transformation is possible. You have only to remain quiet and undisturbed and let the higher Force work to change this obscure physical nature.

*

When one has the cosmic consciousness, one can feel the cosmic Self as one's own self, one can feel one with other beings in the cosmos, one can feel all the forces of Nature as moving in oneself, all selves as one's own self. There is no why except that it is so, since all is the One.

*

When one speaks of the divine spark, one is thinking of the soul as a portion of the Divine which has descended from above into the manifestation rather than of something which has separated itself from the cosmos. It is the nature that has formed itself out of the cosmic forces – mind out of cosmic mind, life out of cosmic life, body out of cosmic Matter.

For the soul there are three realisations: – (1) the realisation of the psychic being and consciousness as the divine element in the evolution; (2) the realisation of the cosmic Self which is one in all; (3) the realisation of the Supreme Divine from which both individual and cosmos have come and of the individual being (Jivatma) as an eternal portion of the Divine.

*

The sadhana is based on the fact that a descent of Forces from the higher planes and an ascent of the lower consciousness to the higher planes are the means of transformation of the lower nature – although naturally it takes time and the complete transformation can only come by the supramental descent.

*

Sadhana is the practice of Yoga. Tapasya is the concentration of the will to get the results of sadhana and to conquer the lower nature. Aradhana is worship of the Divine, love, self-surrender, aspiration to the Divine, calling the name, prayer. Dhyana is inner concentration of the consciousness, meditation, going inside in Samadhi. Dhyana, Tapasya and Aradhana are all parts of sadhana.

*

A pure mind means a mind quiet and free from thoughts of a useless or disturbing character.

*

When one follows after the impersonal Self, one is moving between two opposite principles – the silence and purity of the impersonal inactive Atman and the activity of the ignorant Prakriti. One can pass into the Self, leaving the ignorant nature or reducing it to silence. Or else, one can live in the peace and freedom of the Self and watch the action of Nature as a witness. Even one may put some sattwic control, by tapasya, over the action of the Prakriti; but the impersonal Self has no power to change or divinise the nature. For that one has to go beyond the impersonal Self and seek after the Divine who is both personal and impersonal and beyond these two aspects. If, however, you practise living in the impersonal Self and can achieve a certain spiritual impersonality, then you grow in equality, purity, peace, detachment, you get the power of living in an inner freedom not touched by the surface movement or struggle of the mental, vital and physical nature, and this becomes a great help when you have to go beyond the impersonal and to change the troubled nature also into something divine.

As for the offering of the actions to the Divine and the vital difficulty it raises, it is not possible to avoid the difficulty – you have to go through and conquer it. For the moment you make this attempt, the vital arises with all its restless imperfections to oppose the change. However, there are three things you can do to alleviate and shorten the difficulty:

1. Detach yourself from this vital-physical – observe it as something not yourself; reject it, refuse your consent to its claims and impulses, but quietly as the witness Purusha whose refusal of sanction must ultimately prevail. This ought not to be difficult for you, if you have already learned to live more and more in the impersonal Self.

2. When you are not in this impersonality, still use your mental will and its power of assent or refusal, – not with a painful struggle, but in the same way, quietly, denying the claims of Desire, till these claims by loss of sanction and assent lose their force of return and become more and more faint and external.

3. If you become aware of the Divine above you or in your heart, call for help, for light and power from there to change the vital itself, and at the same time insist upon this vital till it itself learns to pray for the change.

Finally, the difficulty will be reduced to its smallest proportions the moment you can by the sincerity of your aspiration to the Divine and your surrender awaken the psychic being in you (the Purusha in the secret heart) so that it will come forward and remain in front and pour its influence on all the movements of the mind, the vital and the physical consciousness. The work of transformation will still have to be done, but from that moment it will no longer be so hard and painful.

*

In the ordinary course of Yoga that physical strength is replaced by a yogic strength or yogic life-force which keeps up the body and makes it work, but in the absence of this force the body is denuded of power, inert and tamasic. This can only be remedied by the whole being opening to Yoga-Shakti in each of its planes – yogic mind-force, yogic life-force, yogic body-force.

*

The first result of the downflow of the overmind forces is very often to exaggerate the ego, which feels itself strong, almost irresistible (though it is not really so), divinised, luminous. The first thing to do, after some experience of the thing, is to get rid of this magnified ego. For that you have to stand back, not allow yourself to be swept in by the movement, but to watch, understand, reject all mixtures, aspire for a purer and yet purer light and action. This can only be done perfectly if the psychic comes forward. The mind and vital, especially the vital, receiving these forces, can with difficulty resist the tendency to seize on and use them for their ego's objects or, which comes practically to the same thing, they mix the demands of the ego with the service of a higher object.

*

Pranava Japa: It is supposed to have a force of its own although that force cannot fully work without the meditation on the meaning. But my experience is that in these things there is no invariable rule and that must depend on the consciousness or the power of response in the sadhak. With some it has no effect, with some it has a rapid and powerful effect even without meditation – for others the meditation is necessary for any effect to come.

*

How is anger completely got rid of?

When it is the psychic that rules all the movements of the being, then it completely disappears and when the equanimity of the higher consciousness takes complete possession of the lower vital. Till then one can establish control, diminish and reduce it to a touch that has no outward effect or a wave that passes without life-expression.

*

Is the subconscient carried into the next life?

No, the subconscient is the instrument for the physical life and disappears. It is too incoherent to be an organized enduring existence.

*

There is in this condition more a sense of having power than real power. There are some mixed and quite relative powers – sometimes a little effective, sometimes ineffective – which could be developed into something real if put under the control of the Divine, surrendered. But the ego comes in, exaggerates these small things, and represents them as something huge and unique, and refuses to surrender. Then the sadhak makes no progress – he wanders about in the jungle of his own imaginations without any discrimination or critical sense, or brings in a play of confused forces he is unable to understand or master.

*

It is because the energy is put forward in the work. But as the peace and contact grow, a double consciousness can develop – one engaged in the work, another behind, silent and observing or turned towards the Divine – in this consciousness the aspiration can be maintained even while the external consciousness is turned towards the work.

*

Is there "wideness" in the psychic?

The wideness comes when one exceeds or begins to exceed the individual consciousness and spread out towards the universal. But the psychic can be active even in the individual consciousness.

*

How does "breaking of the Veil" occur?

It comes of itself with the pressure of the sadhana. It can also be brought about by specific concentration and effort.

It is certainly better if the psychic is conscious and active before there is the removing of the veil or screen between the individual and the universal consciousness which comes when the inner being is brought forward in all its wideness. For then there is much less danger of the difficulties of what I have called the Intermediate Zone.

*

Impersonality in itself is not the Divine. All these mistakes can be and are made by many who claim to be in an impersonalised consciousness. A force may be universal but may be also a wrong force: many think they are impersonal and free from ego because they are obeying a force or something bigger than their own personality – but that force or that something may be quite other than the Divine and it may hold them by something in their personality and ego.

*

There is only one Force or Energy here in reality; what is called the individual energy does not belong to the individual, but to the one universal Power.

In the one infinite Energy itself a distinction has to be made between the Divine Force that descends from above the mind and the inferior universal Energy with all its different forms, movements, waves and currents that come into you from outside. The inferior Energy proceeds from the Divine Shakti, but it has fallen from the truth of its source and has no longer its direct guidance.

When these universal energies come into touch with the Divine Force, rise to meet it and allow it to take hold of them and occupy and change them, then they are purified and uplifted and transformed and become a movement of the Divine Force.

When they are not in touch with the Divine Force, not obedient to it, but act for themselves, they are unenlightened, erring, impure, mixed and confused – powers of the Ignorance.

Always, therefore, keep in touch with the Divine Force. The best thing for you is to do that simply and allow it to do its own work; wherever necessary, it will take hold of the inferior energies and purify them; at other times it will empty you of them and fill you with itself. But if you let your mind take the lead and discuss and decide what is to be done, you will lose touch with the Divine Force and the lower energies will begin to act for themselves and all go into confusion and a wrong movement.

It is still worse to try to draw these lower universal energies from those around you and keep up with them a vital interchange; what gain can there be in that? On the contrary, it will lead to greater confusion and even bring in all kinds of mischief and trouble.

Often the association of these universal energies with others is a mistake of your mind. Your mind is seeking always to fix them on to somebody, and often it fixes on one or another at random or else according to old experiences which are no longer valid. For instance, what you call X's force was not his, but a universal hostile force which used X at one time and, owing to a continued association in your mind, still presents itself to you as his, but may now no longer have anything to do with him. By keeping up the old association, you simply give greater opportunity for this undesirable energy to come upon you.

Follow always the one rule, to open yourself directly to the Divine Force and not to others; if you keep in touch with it, all else will progressively arrange itself.

*

There can be no physical life without an order and rhythm. When this order is changed, it must be in obedience to an inner growth and not for the sake of external novelty. It is only a certain part of the surface lower vital nature which seeks always external change and novelty for its own sake.

It is by a constant inner growth that one can find a constant newness and unfailing interest in life. There is no other satisfying way.

*

What you felt about replacement is quite true. The transformation proceeds to a large extent by a taking away or throwing out of the old superficial self and its movements and replacing them by a new deeper self and its true action.

It does not matter if the higher feelings, devotion etc. seem to you sometimes like an influence or colouring. It looks like that when you feel yourself in the external physical or outer vital or outer mind. These feelings really are those of your inmost self, your soul, the psychic in you and when you are in the psychic consciousness they become normal and natural. But when your consciousness shifts and becomes more external, then these workings of the soul or of the divine consciousness are felt as themselves external, as merely an influence. All the same, you have to open yourself to them constantly and they will then more and more either soak in steadily or come in successive waves or floods and go on till they have filled the mind, the vital, the body. You will then feel them always as not only normal but as part of your very self and the true substance of your nature.

*

In the ordinary condition of the body if you oblige the body to do too much work, it can do with the support of vital force. But as soon as the work is done, the vital force withdraws and then the body feels fatigue. If this is done too much and for too long a time, there may be a breakdown of health and strength under the overstrain. Rest is then needed for recovery.

If however the mind and the vital get the habit of opening to the Mother's Force, they are then supported by the Force and may even be fully filled with it – the Force does the work and the body feels no strain or fatigue before or after. But even then, unless the body itself is open and can absorb and keep the Force, sufficient rest in between the work is absolutely necessary. Otherwise although the body may go on for a very long time, yet in the end there can be a danger of a collapse.

The body can be sustained for a long time when there is the full influence and there is a single-minded faith and call in the mind and the vital; but if the mind or the vital is disturbed by other influences or opens itself to forces which are not the Mother's, then there will be a mixed condition and there will be sometimes strength, sometimes fatigue, exhaustion or illness or a mixture of the two at the same time.

Finally, if not only the mind and the vital, but the body also is open and can absorb the Force, it can do extraordinary things in the way of work without breaking down. Still even then rest is necessary. That is why we insist on those who have the impulse of work keeping a proper balance between rest and labour.

A complete freedom from fatigue is possible, but that comes only when there is a complete transformation of the law of the body by the full descent of a supramental Force into the earth-nature.

*

The consciousness of the mind, life, body in each person is ordinarily shut up in itself; it is narrow, not wide, sees itself as the centre of everything, judges all things according to its own impressions – it does not know anything as it really is. But when by Yoga one begins to open to the true consciousness, then this barrier begins to break down. One feels the mind grow wider, even in the end the physical consciousness grows wider and wider, until you feel all things in yourself, yourself one with all things. You then become one with the Mother's universal Consciousness.

That is why you feel the mind becoming wide. But also there is much above the human mind and it is this which you feel like a world above your head. All these are the ordinary experiences of our Yoga. It is only a beginning. But in order that it may go on developing, you must become more and more quiet, more and more able to hold whatever comes without getting too eager and excited. Peace and calmness are the first thing, and with it wideness – in the peace you can bear whatever love or Ananda comes, whatever strength comes or whatever knowledge.

*

Chit is the pure consciousness, as in Sat-Chit-Ananda.

Chitta is the stuff of mixed mental-vital-physical consciousness out of which arise the movements of thoughts, emotion, sensation, impulse, etc. It is these that in the Patanjali system have to be stilled altogether so that the consciousness may be immobile and go into Samadhi.

Our Yoga has a different function. The movements of the ordinary consciousness have to be quieted and into the quietude there has to be brought down a higher consciousness and its powers which will transform the nature.

*

If you suppress the Chittavrittis, you will have no movements of the Chitta at all; all will be immobile until you remove the suppression or will be so immobile that there cannot be anything else than immobility.

If you still them, the Chitta will be quiet, whatever movements there are will not disturb the quietude.

If you control or master, then the Chitta will be immobile

when you want, active when you want, and its action will be such that what you wish to get rid of, will go, only what you accept as true and useful will come.

*

The negative means are not evil; they are useful for their object which is to get away from life. But from the positive point of view, they are disadvantageous, because they get rid of the powers of the being instead of divinising them for the transformation of life.

*

What has been put into the vital receptacle by life can be got out by reversing it, turning it towards the Divine and not towards yourself. You will then find that the vital is as excellent an instrument as it is a bad master.

*

There is no harm in concentrating sometimes in the heart and sometimes above the head. But concentration in either place does not mean keeping the attention fixed on a particular spot; you have to take your station of consciousness in either place and concentrate there not on the place, but on the Divine. This can be done with eyes shut or with eyes open, according as it best suits you.

You can concentrate on the sun, but to concentrate on the Divine is better than to concentrate on the sun.

*

The mere intensity of the force does not show that it is a bad power; the Divine Force often works with a great intensity. Everything depends on the nature of the force and its working: what does it do, what seems to be its purpose? If it works to purify or open the system, or brings with it light or peace, or prepares the change of the thought, ideas, feelings, character in the sense of a turning towards a higher consciousness, then it is the right force. If it is dark or obscure or perturbs the being with rajasic or egoistic suggestions or excites the lower nature, then it is an adverse force.

*

Why should you think the Mother does not approve of expression, – provided it is the right expression of the right thing, – or suppose that silence and true expression are contradictory? The truest expression comes out of an absolute inner silence. The spiritual silence is not a mere emptiness; nor is it indispensable to abstain from all activity in order to find it.

*

When a higher force comes down into a lower plane, it is diminished and modified by the inferior substance, lesser power and more mixed movements of that lower plane. Thus, if the Overmind Power works through the illumined mind, only part of its truth and freedom manifests and becomes effective – so much only as can get through this less receptive consciousness. And even what gets through is less true, mixed with other matter, less overmental, more easily modified into something that is part truth, part error. When this diminished indirect force descends further down into the mind and vital, it has still something of the creative Overmind Truth in it, but gets very badly mixed with mental and vital formations that disfigure it and make it half effective only, sometimes ineffective.

*

It is (sometimes directly, sometimes indirectly) by the power of the Overmind releasing the mind from its close partitions that the cosmic consciousness opens in the seeker and he becomes aware of the cosmic spirit and the play of the cosmic forces.

It is from or at least through the Overmind plane that the original prearrangement of things in this world is effected; for from it the determining vibrations come. But there are corresponding movements on all the planes, the mind, the vital, the physical even, and it is possible in a very clear or illumined condition of the lower consciousness to become aware of these movements and understand the plan of things and be either a conscious instrument or even, to a limited extent a determinant Will or Force. But the stuff of the lower planes always mixes with the Overmind forces and diminishes or even falsifies and perverts their truth and power.

It is even possible for the Overmind to transmit to the lower planes of consciousness something of the supramental Light; but, so long as the Supermind does not directly manifest, its Light is modified in the Overmind itself and still further modified in the application by the needs, the demands, the circumscribing possibilities of the individual nature. The success of this diminished and modified Light, e.g., in purifying the physical, cannot be immediate and absolute as the full and direct supramental action would be; it is still relative, conditioned by the individual nature and the balance of the universal forces, resisted by adverse powers, baulked of its perfect result by the unwillingness of the lower workings to cease, limited either in its scope or in its efficacy by the want of a complete consent in the physical nature.

*

The cosmic consciousness does not belong to Overmind in especial; it covers all the planes.

Man is shut up at present in his surface individual consciousness and knows the world (or rather the surface of it) only through his outward mind and senses and by interpreting their contacts with the world. By Yoga there can open in him a consciousness which becomes one with that of the world; he becomes directly aware of a universal Being, universal states, universal Force and Power, universal Mind, Life, Matter and lives in conscious relations with these things. He is then said to have cosmic consciousness.

*

To fix a precise time is impossible except in the two regions of certitude – the pure material which is the field of mathematical certitudes and the Supramental which is the field of divine certitudes. In the planes in between where life has its word to say and things have to evolve under shock and stress, Time and Energy are too much in a flux and apt to kick against the rigour of a prefixed date or programme.

FAITH

Have faith in the Divine, in the Divine Grace, in the truth of the sadhana, in the eventual triumph of the spirit over its mental and vital and physical difficulties, in the Path and the Guru, in the experience of things other than are written in the philosophy of Haeckel or Huxley or Bertrand Russell, because if these things are not true, there is no meaning in Yoga.

*

The abnormal abounds in this physical world, the super-normal is there also. In these matters, apart from any question of faith, any truly rational man with a free mind (not tied up like the rationalists or so-called free-thinkers at every point with the triple cords of *a priori* irrational disbelief) must not cry out at once, "Humbug! Falsehood!" but suspend judgment until he has the necessary experience and knowledge. To deny in ignorance is no better than to affirm in ignorance.

*

The faith in spiritual things that is asked of the sadhak is not an ignorant but a luminous faith, a faith in light and not in darkness. It is called blind by the sceptical intellect because it refuses to be guided by outer appearances or seeming facts, – for it looks for the truth behind, – and because it does not walk on the crutches of proof and evidence. It is an intuition, an intuition not only waiting for experience to justify it, but leading towards experience. If I

believe in self-healing, I shall after a time find out the way
to heal myself. If I have a faith in transformation, I can end
by laying my hand on and unravelling the process of
transformation. But if I begin with doubt and go on with
more doubt, how far am I likely to go on the journey?

*

Faith does not depend upon experience; it is something
that is there before experience. When one starts the Yoga,
it is not usually on the strength of experience, but on the
strength of faith. It is so not only in Yoga and the spiritual life, but in ordinary life also. All men of action, dis-
coverers, inventors, creators of knowledge proceed by faith
and, until the proof is made or the thing done, they go on in
spite of disappointment, failure, disproof, denial because
of something in them that tells them that this is the truth,
the thing that must be followed and done. Ramakrishna
even went so far as to say, when asked whether blind faith
was not wrong, that blind faith was the only kind to have,
for faith is either blind or it is not faith but something
else – reasoned inference, proved conviction or ascertained
knowledge.

Faith is the soul's witness to something not yet manifested, achieved or realised, but which yet the Knower
within us, even in the absence of all indications, feels to be
true or supremely worth following or achieving. This thing
within us can last even when there is no fixed belief in the
mind, even when the vital struggles and revolts and refuses.
Who is there that practises the Yoga and has not his
periods, long periods of disappointment and failure and
disbelief and darkness? But there is something that sustains
him and even goes on in spite of himself, because it feels

that what it followed after was yet true and it more than feels, it knows. The fundamental faith in Yoga is this, inherent in the soul, that the Divine exists and the Divine is the one thing to be followed after – nothing else in life is worth having in comparison with that. So long as a man has that faith, he is marked for the spiritual life and I will say that, even if his nature is full of obstacles and crammed with denials and difficulties, and even if he has many years of struggle, he is marked out for success in the spiritual life.

It is this faith that you need to develop – a faith which is in accordance with reason and common sense – that if the Divine exists and has called you to the Path (as is evident), then there must be a Divine Guidance behind and through and in spite of all difficulties you will arrive. Not to listen to the hostile voices that suggest failure or to the voices of impatient, vital haste that echo them, not to believe that because great difficulties are there, there can be no success or that because the Divine has not yet shown himself he will never show himself, but to take the position that everyone takes when he fixes his mind on a great and difficult goal, "I will go on till I succeed – all difficulties notwithstanding." To which the believer in the Divine adds, "The Divine exists, my following after the Divine cannot fail. I will go on through everything till I find him."

*

I do not ask "undiscriminating faith" from anyone, all I ask is fundamental faith, safeguarded by a patient and quiet discrimination – because it is these that are proper to the consciousness of a spiritual seeker and it is these that I have myself used and found that they removed all necessity for the quite gratuitous dilemma of "either you must doubt everything supraphysical or be entirely credulous", which is the stock-in-trade of the materialist argument. Your doubt, I see, constantly returns to the charge with a repetition of this formula in spite of my denial – which supports my assertion that Doubt cannot be convinced, because by its very nature it does not want to be convinced; it keeps repeating the old ground always.

*

I do not see how the method of faith in the cells can be likened to eating a slice of the moon. Nobody ever got a slice of the moon, but the healing by faith in the cells is an actual fact and a law of Nature and has been demonstrated often enough even apart from Yoga. The way to get faith and all things else is to insist on having them and refuse to flag or despair or give up until one has them – it is the way by which everything has been got since this difficult earth began to have thinking and aspiring creatures upon it. It is to open always, always to the Light and turn one's back on the darkness. It is to refuse the voices that say persistently, "You cannot, you shall not, you are incapable, you are the puppet of a dream," – for these are the enemy voices, they cut one off from the result that was coming, by their strident clamour and then triumphantly point to the barrenness of the result as a proof of their thesis. The difficulty of the endeavour is a known thing, but the difficult is not the impossible – it is the difficult that has always been accomplished and the conquest of difficulties makes up all that is valuable in the earth's history. In the spiritual endeavour also it shall be so.

You have only to set about resolutely slaying the

Rakshasa and the doors will open to you as they have done
to many others who were held up by their own mind or vital
nature.

LOVE – BHAKTI – EMOTION

In the way of *ahaitukī bhakti*, everything can be made a means – poetry and music, for instance, become not merely poetry and music and not merely even an expression of Bhakti, but themselves a means of bringing the experience of love and Bhakti. Meditation itself becomes not an effort of mental concentration, but a flow of love and adoration and worship.

*

The very object of Yoga is a change of consciousness – it is by getting a new consciousness or by unveiling the hidden consciousness of the true being within and progressively manifesting and perfecting it that one gets first the contact and then the union with the Divine. Ananda and Bhakti are part of that deeper consciousness and it is only when one lives in it and grows in it that Ananda and Bhakti can be permanent. Till then, one can only get experiences of Ananda and Bhakti, but not the constant and permanent state. But the state of Bhakti and constantly growing surrender does not come to all at an early stage of the sadhana; many, most indeed, have a long journey of purification and Tapasya to go through before it opens, and experiences of this kind, at first rare and interspersed, afterwards frequent, are the landmarks of their progress. It depends on certain conditions, which have nothing to do with superior or inferior Yoga-capacity, but rather with a predisposition in the heart to open, as you say, to the Sun of the Divine Influence.

*

Absence of love and fellow-feeling is not necessary for nearness to the Divine; on the contrary, a sense of closeness and oneness with others is a part of the divine consciousness into which the sadhak enters by nearness to the Divine and the feeling of oneness with the Divine. An entire rejection of all relations is indeed the final aim of the Mayavadin, and in the ascetic Yoga an entire loss of all relations of friendship and affection and attachment to the world and its living beings would be regarded as a promising sign of advance towards liberation, *mokṣa*; but even there, I think, a feeling of oneness and unattached spiritual sympathy for all is at least a penultimate stage, like the compassion of the Buddhist, before the turning to Moksha or Nirvana. In this Yoga the feeling of unity with others, love, universal joy and Ananda are an essential part of the liberation and perfection which are the aim of the sadhana.

On the other hand, human society, human friendship, love, affection, fellow-feeling are mostly and usually – not entirely or in all cases – founded on a vital basis and are ego-held at their centre. It is because of the pleasure of being loved, the pleasure of enlarging the ego by contact, mutual penetration of spirit with another, the exhilaration of the vital interchange which feeds their personality that men usually love – and there are also other and still more selfish motives that mix with this essential movement. There are of course higher spiritual, psychic, mental, vital elements that come in or can come in; but the whole thing is very mixed, even at its best. This is the reason why at a certain stage with or without apparent reason the world and life and human society and relations and philanthropy (which is as ego-ridden as the rest) begin to pall. There is sometimes an ostensible reason – a disappointment of the surface vital, the withdrawal of affection by others, the perception that those loved or men generally are not what one thought them to be and a host of other causes; but often the cause is a secret disappointment of some part of the inner being, not translated or not well translated into the mind because it expected from these things something which they cannot give. It is the case with many who turn or are pushed to the spiritual life. For some it takes the form of a *vairāgya* which drives them towards ascetic indifference and gives the urge towards Moksha. For us, what we hold to be necessary is that the mixture should disappear and that the consciousness should be established on a purer level (not only spiritual and psychic but a purer and higher mental, vital, physical consciousness) in which there is not this mixture. There one would feel the true Ananda of oneness and love and sympathy and fellowship, spiritual and self-existent in its basis but expressing itself through the other parts of the nature. If that is to happen, there must obviously be a change; the old form of these movements must drop off and leave room for a new and higher self to disclose its own way of expression and realisation of itself and of the Divine through these things – that is the inner truth of the matter.

I take it therefore that the condition you describe is a period of transition and change, negative in its beginning, as these movements often are at first, so as to create a vacant space for the new positive to appear and live in it and fill it. But the vital, not having a long continued or at all sufficient or complete experience of what is to fill the vacancy, feels only the loss and regrets it even while another part of the being, another part even of the vital, is ready to let go what is disappearing and does not yearn to keep it. If it were not for this movement of the vital, (which in your case has been very strong and large and avid of life),

the disappearance of these things would, at least after the
first sense of void, bring only a feeling of peace, relief and a
still expectation of greater things. What is intended in the
first place to fill the void was indicated in the peace and joy
which came to you as the touch of Shiva – naturally, this
would not be all but a beginning, a basis for a new self, a
new consciousness, an activity of a greater nature; as I told
you, it is a deep spiritual calm and peace that is the only
stable foundation for a lasting Bhakti and Ananda. In that
new consciousness there would be a new basis for relations
with others; for an ascetic dryness or isolated loneliness
cannot be your spiritual destiny since it is not consonant
with your Swabhava which is made for joy, largeness,
expansion, a comprehensive movement of the life-force.
Therefore do not be discouraged; wait upon the purifying
movement of Shiva.

*

Emotion is a good element in Yoga; but the emotional
desire becomes easily a cause of perturbation and an
obstacle.

Turn your emotions towards the Divine, aspire for their
purification; they will then become a help on the way and
no longer a cause of suffering.

Not to kill emotion, but to turn it towards the Divine is
the right way of the Yoga.

But it must become pure, founded upon spiritual peace
and joy, capable of being transmuted into Ananda. Equality
and calm in the mind and vital parts, an intense psychic
emotion in the heart can perfectly go together.

Awake by your aspiration the psychic fire in the heart
that burns steadily towards the Divine – that is the one way
to liberate and fulfil the emotional nature.

COLOURS – SYMBOLS – VISIONS

The frequent seeing of lights such as those he writes of in his letter is usually a sign that the seer is not limited by his outward surface or waking consciousness but has a latent capacity (which can be perfected by training and practice) for entering into the experiences of the inner consciousness of which most people are unaware but which open by the practice of Yoga. By this opening one becomes aware of subtle planes of experience and worlds of existence other than the material. For the spiritual life a still further opening is required into an inmost consciousness by which one becomes aware of the Self and Spirit, the Eternal and the Divine.

*

The power of occult seeing is there in every one, mostly latent, often near the surface, sometimes but much more rarely already on the surface. If one practises *trāṭak*, it is pretty certain to come out sooner or later, – though some have a difficulty and with them it takes time; those in whom it comes out at once have had all the time this power of occult vision near the surface and it emerges at the first direct pressure.

The rays which you saw the trees giving out are there always, only they are veiled to the ordinary material vision. I said the blue and gold together indicated the combined presence of Krishna and Durga-Mahakali; but gold and yellow have different significances. Yellow in the indication of forces signifies the thinking mind, *buddhi* and the pink (modified here into a light vermilion) is a psychic colour; the combination probably meant the psychic in the mental.

In interpreting these phenomena you must remember that all depends on the order of things which the colours indicate in any particular case. There is an order of significances in which they indicate various psychological dynamisms, e.g., faith, love, protection, etc.; there is another order of significances in which they indicate the aura or the activity of divine beings, Krishna, Mahakali, Radha or else of other superhuman beings; there is another in which they indicate the aura around objects or living persons – and that does not exhaust the list of possibilities. A certain knowledge, experiences, growing intuition are necessary to perceive in each case the true significance. Observation and exact description are also very necessary; for sometimes people say, for instance, yellow when they mean gold or vice versa; there are besides different possible meanings for different shades of the same colour. Again, if you see colour near or round a person or by looking at him or her, it does not necessarily indicate that person's aura; it may be something else near him or around him. In some cases it may have nothing to do with the person or object you look at, which may serve merely the purpose of a background or a point of concentration – as when you see colours on a wall or by looking at a bright object.

*

As for the exact symbolism of colours, it is not always easy to define exactly, because it is not rigid and precise, but complex, the meaning varying with the field, the combinations, the character and shades of the colour, the play of forces. A certain kind of yellow, for instance, is supposed by many occultists to indicate the *buddhi*, the intellect, and it often has that sense, but occurring among a play of vital forces it could not always be so interpreted – that would be too rigid. Here all one can say is that the blue (the particular blue seen, not every blue) indicated the response to the Truth; the green – or *this* green – is very usually associated with Life and a generous emanation or action of forces – often of emotional life-force, and it is probably this that it would indicate here.

*

Colour and light are always close to each other – colour being more indicative, light more dynamic. Colour incandescent becomes light.

Gold indicates at its most intense something from the Supramental, otherwise Overmind truth or intuitive truth deriving ultimately from the Supramental Truth Consciousness.

*

The golden light is usually a light from the Supermind – a light of Truth-Knowledge (it may sometimes be the supramental Truth-Knowledge turned into overmind or intuitive truth). Orange often indicates occult power. You have a strong power of (subjective) creative formation, mostly, I think, in the mental but partly too on the vital plane. This kind of formative faculty can be used for objective results if accompanied by a sound knowledge of the occult forces and their workings; but by itself it results more often in one's building up an inner world of one's own in which you can live very well satisfied, as long as you live in yourself, apart from any close contact with external physical life; but it does not stand the test of objective experience.

*

That means the light of the divine consciousness (the Mother's Consciousness, white light) in the vital. Blue is the higher mind, gold the divine Truth. So it is the vital with the light of the higher mind and the divine Truth in it emanating the Mother's light.

*

That is some obstacle in the mind breaking under the pressure of Force, and each time there is a flash and a movement of the Force.

*

The star is always a promise of the Light to come; the star changes into a sun when there is the descent of the Light.

*

The Lights one sees in concentration are the lights of various powers or forces and often lights that come down from the higher consciousness.

The violet light is that of the Divine Compassion (*karuṇā* – Grace) – the white light is the light of the Mother (the Divine Consciousness) in which all others are contained and from which they can be manifested.

Purple is the colour of vital power. "Red" depends on

the character of the colour, for there are many reds – this may be the colour of the physical consciousness.

*

The vision of the Light and the vision of the Lord in the form of Jagannath are both of them indications that he has the capacity for Yoga and that there is a call of the Divine on his inner being. But capacity is not enough; there must be also the will to seek after the Divine and courage and persistence in following the path. Fear is the first thing that must be thrown away and, secondly, the inertia of the outer being which has prevented him from responding to the call.

The Light is the light of the Divine Consciousness. The aim of this Yoga is first to come into contact with this consciousness and then to live in its light and allow the light to transform the whole nature, so that the being may live in union with the Divine and the nature become a field for the action of the divine Knowledge, the divine Power and the divine Ananda.

He can succeed in this only if he makes it the supreme object of his life and is prepared to subordinate everything else to this one aim. Otherwise all that can be done is only to make some preparation in this life – a first contact and some preliminary spiritual change in part of the nature.

*

(a) It means the essential Force of the Mother (diamond light).

(b) The diamond light proceeds from the heart of the Divine Consciousness and it brings the opening of the Divine Consciousness wherever it goes.

(c) The Mother's descent with the diamond light is the sanction of the Supreme Power to the movement in you.

(d) The Mother's diamond light is a light of absolute purity and power.

(e) The diamond light is the central consciousness and force of the Divine.

*

In each plane there is an objective as well as a subjective side. It is not the physical plane and life alone that are objective.

When you have the power of formation of which I spoke, whatever is suggested to the mind, the mind constructs and establishes a form of it in itself. But this power can cut two ways; it may tempt the mind to construct mere images of the reality and mistake them for the reality itself. It is one of the many dangers of a too active mind.

You make a formation in your mind or on the vital plane in yourself – it is a kind of creation, but subjective only; it affects only your own mental or vital being. You can create by ideas, thought-forms, images, a whole world in yourself or for yourself; but it stops there.

Some have the power of making consciously formations that go out and affect the mind, actions, vital movements, external lives of others. These formations may be destructive as well as creative.

Finally, there is the power to make formations that become effective realities in the earth-consciousness here, in its mind, life, physical existence. That is what we usually mean by creation.

*

A sensation of coolness indicates usually some touch or descent of peace. It is felt as very cold by the human vital because the latter is always in a fever of restlessness.

*

The serpent is a symbol of force, very often a hostile or evil force of the vital plane.

The sea is a symbol of a plane of consciousness.

The white light is a manifestation of pure divine force descending from one of the truth-planes leading to the supramental.

*

When you see a square, that is a symbol of complete creation; when you see a buffalo rushing upon you and missing and feel you have escaped a great danger, that is a transcription. Something actually happened of which the buffalo's ineffectual rush was your mind's transcription – the rush of some hostile force represented by the buffalo.

*

The arrow is the symbol of the Force which goes to its aim. Gold=the Truth, Yellow=the mind, Green=the vital energy. The arrow of the spiritual Truth using the mind and the vital energy.

*

All visions have a significance of one kind or another. This power of vision is very important for the Yoga and should not be rejected although it is not the most important thing – for the most important thing is the change of the consciousness. All other powers like this of vision should be developed without attachment as parts and aids of the Yoga.

*

Gods. These are Powers that stand above the world and transmit the divine workings.

Brahma is the Power of the Divine that stands behind formation and creation.

Ganesh is the Power that removes obstacles by the force of Knowledge.

Kartikeya represents victory over the hostile powers.

*

Those who were with Krishna were in all appearance men like other men. They spoke and acted with each other as men with men and were not thought of by those around them as gods. Krishna himself was known by most as a man – only a few worshipped him as the Divine.

*

The boy with the flute is Sri Krishna, the Lord descended into the world-play from the divine Ananda; his flute is the music of the call which seeks to transform the lower ignorant play of mortal life and bring into it and establish in its place the Lila of his divine Ananda. It was the psychic being in you that heard the call and followed after it.

*

The vision simply means that when you clutch at anything and try to make it your own with an egoistic sense of possession, then however beautiful and wonderful it may be, it loses its value and becomes ordinary.

*

The visions you describe are those which come in the earliest stages of sadhana. At this stage most of the things seen are formations of the mental plane and it is not always possible to put on them a precise significance; for, they depend on the individual mind of the Sadhak. At a later stage the power of vision becomes important for the sadhana, but at first one has to go on without attaching excessive importance to the details – until the consciousness develops more. The opening of the consciousness to the Divine Light and Truth and Presence is always the one important thing in the Yoga.

*

Dreams or visions on the vital plane are usually either
(1) symbolic vital visions
(2) actual occurrences on the vital plane
(3) formations of the vital mind, either of the dreamer or of some one else with whom he contacts in sleep or of powers or beings of that plane. No great reliance can be put on this kind of experience, even the first having only a relative or suggestive value, while the second and third are often quite misleading.

*

(1) The lid of the skull opening means that the mental being has opened to the Divine Light, and the flames indicate aspirations filled with the Light arising to join the mental part to what is above Mind.

(2) The Divine Light from above is of various colours. White is the divine Power of purity, blue the light of the spiritual consciousness, gold the hue of the supramental knowledge or of knowledge from the intermediate planes.

(3) OM (golden) rising to the sky means the cosmic consciousness supramentalised and rising towards the transcendent Consciousness.

(1) and (2) indicate either something that is happening at present or a potentiality that is trying to materialise. (3) symbolises the process of the Yoga which will be followed if this potentiality is realised and pursued to its natural goal.

GLOSSARY OF SANSKRIT TERMS

Proper names have been omitted from the glossary. All words are listed here in their strict transliterated form; Sri Aurobindo's spelling is indicated where it differs significantly from this transliteration. Definitions are given in Sri Aurobindo's own words as far as possible.

abhyāsa – steady practice.

ādhār(a) – vessel, receptacle; the system of mind, life and body considered as a receptacle of the spiritual consciousness and force.

ahaitukī – motiveless, spontaneous.

ājñācakra (Ajna Chakra) – the centre between the eye-brows which governs the dynamic mind, will, vision, mental formation.

ānanda – bliss, delight; the divine or spiritual bliss.

ānandamaya – blissful.

anityam asukham – transient and unhappy.

anumantā – giver of the sanction.

ārādhanā – worship of the Divine.

ātman – true self.

bhakta – devotee.

bhakti – devotion.

brahman – Spirit.

buddheḥ parataḥ – above the thinking mind.

buddhi – thinking mind.

cakra (Chakra) – any one of the seven psychological centres in the subtle body.

cit (Chit) – pure consciousness; the universal conscious-stuff of existence.

citta (Chitta) – mind-stuff.

cittavṛtti (Chittavritti) – movement of the mind.

damana – suppression.

devī – Goddess.

dharma – law of action.

dhyāna – meditation.

guru – spiritual teacher.

guruvāda – the doctrine that stresses the indispensability of the *guru* to the spiritual seeker.

īśvarakoṭi (Ishwarakoti) – those who get to the integral Reality and can therefore combine the Ascent with the Descent.

jaḍa – inert, mechanical, inconscient.

jīva – living creature; individual spirit, soul in Nature.

jīvakoṭi – those who describe only the curve from Matter through Mind into the silent *brahman*.

jīvanmukta – living liberated man.

jīvātmā – the individual self; the *ātman*, spirit or eternal self of the living being.

jñāna – wisdom; self-knowledge.

karmayoga – the system of spiritual discipline which takes work (dedicated to the Divine) as its basis.

karuṇā – compassion; Grace.

laya – dissolution of the individual being; merging in the one Self-Existence.

līlā – cosmic Play.

māyāvādin – one who holds the doctrine that the world is an illusion (*māyā*); Illusionist.

mokṣa (Moksha) – spiritual liberation from the sense of personal being; release from cosmic existence.

mūlādhār(a) – the centre at the base of the spine which governs the physical down to the subconscient.

nirvāṇa – spiritual extinction of the separate individual self.

om – the sound-symbol of the *brahman*.

paṇḍit(a) – scholar, learned man.

pātāla – the nether world.

prakṛti (Prakriti) – Nature, the active and executive Energy, as distinguished from the witnessing and sustaining soul or conscious being.

prāṇa – life-force; the nervous energy, the vital breath, the half-mental, half-material dynamism which links mind and matter.

praṇava japa – repetition of *om*.

prārabdha karma – the chain of action and result already set in motion; the unfulfilled effects of past lives.

puruṣa (Purusha) – the soul or conscious being supporting the action of Nature.

puruṣottama (Purushottama) – the Supreme Being.

rajas – one of the three gunas, fundamental qualities or modes of Nature; the kinetic principle in Nature characterised by desire, action and passion.

rākṣasa – giant power of darkness; being of the middle vital plane in opposition to the Gods.

ripu – (inner) enemy.

saccidānanda (Sachchidananda, Sat-Chit-Ananda) – the Supreme Reality as self-existent Being, Consciousness and Bliss.

sādhak(a) – one who practises the discipline of *yoga*.

sādhanā – the discipline of *yoga* as a means of realisation; practice of the *yoga*.

sahasradal(a) – the thousand-petalled lotus above the head, the higher consciousness centre.

śakti (Shakti) – Force; the Divine Power, the Conscious Force of the Divine.

samādhi – Yogic trance.

samatā – equality of soul, equanimity founded on the sense of the one Self, the one Divine everywhere.

saṁsāra – rebirth in the unstable life of the universe.

saṁskāra – impression, association, fixed notion, habitual reaction formed by one's past.

sannyāsī – ascetic.

śāstra (Shastra) – the moral and social code.

Sat-Chit-Ananda – see *saccidānanda*.

sattva (sattwa) – one of the three gunas, fundamental qualities or modes of Nature; the principle of light and harmony in Nature.

Shakti – see *śakti*.

Shastra – see *śāstra*.

siddhi – perfection; the accomplishment of the aims of *yoga*.

sūkṣma deha – the subtle body.

śūnya – void.

svabhāva (Swabhava) – inner nature, spiritual temperament, essential character.

svarūpa – self-form; the eternal form of the Divinity.

Swabhava – see *svabhāva*.

tamas – one of the three gunas, fundamental qualities or modes of Nature; the principle of obscurity and inertia in Nature.

tapas – concentration of power of consciousness; the principle of spiritual power and force in the higher or divine Nature.

tapasyā – spiritual effort by concentration of the energies in a spiritual discipline or process.

trāṭak(a) – concentrating the vision on a single point or object, preferably a luminous object.

vairāgya – disgust with the world.

vijñāna – comprehensive consciousness; ideal mind or supermind.

vṛtti (vritti) – functioning.

yoga – union with the Divine; the discipline by which one enters through an awakening into an inner and higher consciousness into that union.

yoga-śakti (Yoga-Shakti) – the Power that comes with the awakening of the inner and higher consciousness.

yogī – one who is established in the realisation of *yoga*.